What You Wish For

poems by

Ruth Bardon

Finishing Line Press
Georgetown, Kentucky

What You Wish For

Copyright © 2023 by Ruth Bardon
ISBN 979-8-88838-151-9 First Edition
All rights reserved under International and Pan-American Copyright Conventions.
No part of this book may be reproduced in any manner whatsoever without written permission from the publisher, except in the case of brief quotations embodied in critical articles and reviews.

Publisher: Leah Huete de Maines
Editor: Christen Kincaid
Cover Art: Mui Joo Wee
Author Photo: Daniel Turbert; Daniel Turbert Photography, LLC
Cover Design: Elizabeth Maines McCleavy

Order online: www.finishinglinepress.com
also available on amazon.com

Author inquiries and mail orders:
Finishing Line Press
PO Box 1626
Georgetown, Kentucky 40324
USA

Table of Contents

The Well	1
Wanting What's Fair	2
Snow White in the Spring	4
Work	5
Red	6
The Fisherman's Wife	7
Cheerleader	9
Hansel	10
Gretel	11
Witch	12
Straw, Gold, Wedding	13
Wonderland	14
Grand Staircase	15
While She Was Sleeping	16
Island	17
Tree Top	18
If I'd Known	19
Mermaid	20
His Mother, Afterwards	21
Rapunzel's Hair	23

for Beth and Daniel

With gratitude to my husband, Mike Casey, for his love and support, and to Kelly Rowe and Christine Hait, who always believed in these poems.

The Well

You stood leaning over its rough rim
searching for your face down below,
but you couldn't even see the water.

The water was something you believed in,
as you believed that the stars
were really enormous suns.

Your wishes scattered like crumbs
on the surface you couldn't see
and stayed there for a while

before they all grew waterlogged
and had to sink slowly, reluctantly,
into the stream below,

a stream like a blue vein
under the skin of the earth,
licking at the rock

that spread in every direction,
flowing under your feet
as you made your way back home.

Then you remembered your wishes
and wished you could take them back
and wondered what damage they'd done.

Wanting What's Fair

I keep the mirror in the hallway
as if it's nothing special

but late at night
when the servants are sleeping
it pulls me close.

I stand before
its serpents and swirls;
my beauty melts
and the mirror speaks.

It's a fluttering curtain,
an open window
brushed by a tree branch.

There's a part of me
that wants that branch
to break under my weight.

The ground would rush up
in a flurry of leaves
as I fly towards it.

There might be apples
like hard red fists

or the branch might hold steady
and let me climb out,
leaving my robe and my crown behind.

Before long, I'd be someone else,
the fruit would be buried
in a blanket of snow,

and the girl would find the robe and crown,
she'd put them away,
or she might put them on,

and then the mirror would speak to her.

Snow White in the Spring

As far as I know, there are five stages:
childhood, which I don't remember;
then cleaning for the men;
next, sleeping—very nice;
now, this shattering;
and I don't know what's next.

The sleep was best, without doubt.
I liked the wreaths of roses,
and I could catch the sound,
if not the sense, of what was said.
Rainy days, sunny days,
animals or not,
my head is a good place to be,
and always there was that feeling
of being loved and cherished
as the men stood watch around me.

Now this, which is something new:
the glass rings with each blow
and breaks into spiny feathers
that tickle their way toward me.
The velvet cushion sparkles
like a field of snow in the sun—
this bier wasn't meant to be broken.

The animals creep away.
The men look at their feet.

Who is this stranger with an axe?
What does he want of me?
Something that starts with a blade,
even if it's followed by a kiss,
can't ever be happy after.

Work

We started whistling
because down in the mine,
it was too dark to see.
We stepped into blackness,
hazarding the dirt
that rolled under our boots.
We scrabbled at the walls
and they crumbled away,
the air, thick and sour,
puckering our lips.
Sound was misshapen;
it bounced around corners
and squeezed its way
along narrow passages,
but we whistled and listened
and mastered that language,
and could tell how near,
how far, how low,
always telling each other
that the gems we found
would bring what we craved,
would bring something radiant,
something like sunlight,
and we'd rise from the ground
like slim young trees,
fluttering
our dark green leaves.

Red

In the poem by Yeats, Anne Gregory wished
that someone could love her for herself—
in vain. They loved her for her hair
as they love me for my hood,
which is even less a part of me,
which could be carelessly left behind,
forgotten on a chair, a table,
tossed like a speck of dirt from a cloth—
then I'd step on the main path
like a squirrel or a bird, blending in,
no longer a berry, a rose, a ruby.
Only God could love Anne,
but God is nowhere in these woods,
so I wear my hood and keep walking,
as instructed by my mother,
wondering what can possibly save me.

The Fisherman's Wife

This is how it works:

the sun shines down
and the green tendrils
stretch upwards
and the shoots
push aside the heavy dirt

and when they feel
the warmth and the light
they climb even higher.

Each spring, the snake
sheds its skin, sloughing off
that old home for a better,
and the bird darts and flashes
from tree to tree
parading its new feathers.

Even the flounder
felt that hunger;
it opened its mouth
over and over and over,

first to breathe,
then to eat,
then to grant wishes,
then to destroy them.

It needed more
than one gulp or one meal
and more than one home.
It swam far
in search of prey,

in search of depth.

But in the end
it laughed at us both:
at my empty husband,
trudging back and forth
with his broken requests

and at me, the only one of us
who lifted her eyes higher
than the dirt floor of our shack
or the slimy thick mud
of the ocean floor.

Cheerleader

What no one ever
ever understands
is that we're working for them,
not for ourselves.
It's always someone else's victory—
put yourself in my shoes:
day after day,
praying for success
that's not your own,
being a particle
in a wave of noise,
or a flash of color,
a pinprick, a dot,
and dreaming
night after night
of that moment
in the locker room
when you look up from the sink
and the person facing you
with the hairspray in her hand
is a big hairy man.

Hansel

Even your sister has lost hope.
The pine needles
that you thought would be compass points
weave together
or break into fragments.
A piece of a bird's nest
can look like a crumb,
but all it is
is a broken house.
The sky is blue,
but that's not helpful.
The moss is everywhere.
The moss is nowhere.

So listen to me:
you have to join
the rest of us now.
You had your turn
in that lucky club
of family, hearth, and bread,
and now you can learn
how to put together
instead of tearing little pieces,
tossing them out,
and wishing
they'll form something new.

Gretel

Hunger was a din
that filled up our ears.

Its fist squeezed us
out of the house.

My brother had plans
but the birds and animals
were as hungry as we were.

To them, we looked
like logs that rolled,
piles of leaves
pushed by the wind.

When we stopped, we slept,
and the next day, a gift—
the sun rose, a marigold
behind the trees.

It pulled us steadily
into its warmth,
into its promise
of sweetness and shelter.

Witch

Daddy was a big help
with my essay and recommendations,
so no surprise that I landed at my first choice
with an invitation to the dean's dinner.
Coming back to the dorm, I was dressed
in heels, and all the others
straggling out in sweaty clothes
and lugging trunks up the stairway,
including some scrumptious boys.
Helpful that it's easy to ask for help,
helpful that I have a fridge
with cold beer and pre-mixed margaritas,
helpful that we're all strangers,
helpful that I'm prettier than the other girls,
but then again,
they're not as hungry as I am,
and not nearly as hard to feed.

Straw, Gold, Wedding

My own name didn't matter—
I was "the miller's daughter,"
a name that's been replaced
by one that's just the same,
meaning "someone's something."
Either way, it feels as if
I never had a christening,
never had an invitation.

We were both nameless once,
you in your funny hide-out,
I working for my father.
I was acquainted with straw,
but knew nothing about gold.

Now you've disappeared,
and though there are gruesome rumors,
I think you're still hopping around,
singing to the trees and your fire
about the riches you'll get.

You kept the necklace and ring,
and I'm left with my story—
in which all I get to do
is be lied about, and shamed,
first the daughter of a vain man,
then the wife of a greedy one,
a man who has no interest
in guessing who I am.

Wonderland

If you were very small,
you could escape.
You could crawl under the quarter round,
hide in electrical outlets.
Outside there are broken nuts and the holes
left by high heels.

If you were very large,
you could spread to a thinness
unimagined
and float above, hidden in plain sight.
You could grow terrible
and swallow your enemies,
licking your lips,
an ocean licking the shoreline.

If you are in between,
neither small nor large,
you hide by thinking hard
and blending in.
You can't outrun
or fly.

You can close your eyes.
You can be a block of wood.
Your fingers are twisted twigs,
your toes are root's eruptions,
you hope to be scenery,
the rustle of leaves,
and the light flickering through them.

Grand Staircase

I found the dust distracting
as I floated up the stairs,
looking at the riser
seven steps above,
seeing only dirt,
dust mice and scuffs,
thinking of the work
one would have to do
to scrub away this mess,
feeling just how strange
the transition, and how wrong
to be there at all—
poised at the top
like a teetering dish
about to drop—
all this nonsense
about the shoe fitting
when what didn't fit
was the prince.

While She was Sleeping

I was dreaming
about traveling the world.
I was by myself.

I was moving through the water
as fast as seagulls fly
on a ship with no sails.

I sat in a metal carriage
with no horses
and the trees raced by.

I was flying above the clouds
and the lights below me
were clusters of fireflies.

Now I sleep at night,
and my dreams are short
and always the same:

my dead father and mother
tearing up the garden
trying to find me.

Island

For a long time
we'd heard rumors
of distant villages.
Strange things
washed up on shore
and were brought to me.
Each time this happened
I ordered my people
to refrain from movement,
to stay silent,
so I could hear the things speak,
so I could pronounce them
good or bad omens.

They never spoke—
which made me wonder
about my powers,
my position,
my future.
So I decreed that henceforth
each silent thing
that the ocean offered
was a talisman
and could not be touched,
upon penalty of death,
and I waited for the time to come,
as I knew it would,

when my wise counsel
would be ignored,
when a small child
would pick something up,
drop it in my hand,
and wait.

Tree Top

Imagine your baby rocking in the tree.
Imagine the people singing below.
Now the wind is blowing.
Now the grasses are waving.
It's the meadow of your childhood,
the same low humming,
and scattered bits of chaff
are dancing in the sunlight
and tickling your legs.

The cradle is rough wood,
not what you'd have picked.
The crowd is looking up now,
their voices growing louder.
The song lulls you to sleep.
You need to be awake.
This is all so wrong,
but it's what happens:
winds blow, people sing, branches spread.

If you could see through the walls
of houses and barns,
you'd see lovers coupling, seeds
being planted, small metal teeth sawing
back and forth, rough calloused hands
hammering nails, splintered ladders
propped against trees, babes
wrapped in woven blankets,

but what you see instead is leaves
that age as you watch, that turn
from lime to ivy to red to sere,
that fall and drift down like snow.

If I'd Known

I'm the one without a story.
I'm the one who just did her duty:
putting on the clothes, standing at the balcony,
standing, eventually, at the altar.
I lay down that night in the high bed
and felt the chill of the room,
watched the dust motes drift
from curtain to heavy curtain,
heard the trumpets fade
as the trumpeters retreated.

The gifts I received
were not transformative.
A princess with a silver bowl
is the same princess, not
something unforeseen
and wonderful in her strangeness.
The apples were merely apples,
the frogs, frogs.

If I'd known, I might have run.
I might have seen in the mirror
the dark hills over my shoulder
like the murky background of a portrait.

I might have made a nest
far off in the woods, with a window
for squirrels and birds and deer
to gather and greet me.
Instead, I stayed, and had my likeness
painted, and painted again,

and stamped on coins
that still exist, resting
on the velvet bottom
of a glass case.

Mermaid

The others hate me
because I'm always clean,
never worry what to wear
or if my thighs look fat,
while they struggle to look good
despite being locked in towers
or scrounging in the woods
or lying awake at night,
thinking about spindles
and christening guests.
Where I live there's no weight,
there are no reflections,
and I'm always sleek,
my smooth hair flowing
over my shoulders;
I'm unburdened, untroubled,
just paddling away
in a clear blue world
that no prince can enter.

His Mother, Afterwards

When the princess kissed him,
he came back,
but the years were not restored.

He never journeyed
to other kingdoms,
hearing strange words

and nodding grandly
as his horse trotted past
the cheering crowds.

He never stole out
of the castle at night,
dressed like a commoner,

to walk the dirt lanes
and talk with his subjects;
he never learned

to hunt, to fight, to rule,
to be skilled in any way,
to move beyond first lessons.

He sat there croaking
and catching flies
year after year

while we all got older.
Each day sank in the water
like a raindrop, blending

and making no difference
to the pond or the fish
while we thirsted.

As bad as it was,
we were better off then,
going down to the river

where we'd curse at witches
and wait together
for the magic we believed in.

Rapunzel's Hair

What matters isn't the length—
or the height of the tower or the smoothness
of the walls, or the number of years
spent alone, not the song, lyrics,
melody, pitch, not the tone of your voice
when your mother comes to call,
not how quick you are to be grateful,
how quick to smile, not your skin,
your looks, not beauty, not charm,
not smarts, not appeal.
What matters is that there's ground outside
for someone to stand on, and later—
someone to stand there

Ruth Bardon grew up in Highland Park, New Jersey, and lived in a number of midwestern cities before firmly settling in Durham, North Carolina. She received an MFA degree from the Iowa Writers Workshop in 1982 and a PhD in English from the University of North Carolina at Chapel Hill in 1995. Her poems have appeared in journals including *Boulevard, The Cincinnati Review, New Ohio Review, Salamander, Moon City Review,* and *The Chattahoochee Review,* and her first chapbook, *Demon Barber,* was published by Main Street Rag in 2020. She is also the author of *Selected Short Stories of William Dean Howells* (Ohio University Press, 1997).

www.ingramcontent.com/pod-product-compliance
Lightning Source LLC
Chambersburg PA
CBHW022128090426
42743CB00008B/1057